MUSEUM GUIDES FOR

Kids

GREEK & ROMAN ART

Ruthie Knapp and Janice Lehmberg

Davis Publications, Inc.
Worcester, Massachusetts

Hello! I'm your tour guide, Rembrandt. This is a painting I did of myself. I have done lots of portraits of myself—about 100, in fact. In 1629 I finished this painting called *Artist in His Studio*. And *I'm* the artist, Rembrandt.

I've spent almost four hundred years trying to finish the painting on the easel. Do I ever need a break!

I am going to hang up my palette with the one you see behind me on the wall and unlatch the door to your right. Then I can join you from time to time as you read this book. I would like to help you look at Greek and Roman art. After all, three centuries of painting have taught me a trick or two!

Rembrandt van Rijn, *Artist in His Studio*, ca. 1629.

© 2000 Janice G. Lehmberg and Ruth C. Knapp
Illustrations © John McIntosh of McIntosh Ink, Inc.
Design: Janis Owens

Printed in the United States of America
ISBN: 0-87192-549-4
10 9 8 7 6 5 4 3 2 1

Front cover: Greek, Attic, *Nolan Amphora,* ca. 450–440 BC. Ceramic, red-figure, h: 13" x d: 6½" (33.2 x 16.7 cm). Bequest of Mrs. Martin Brimmer, Courtesy Museum of Fine Arts, Boston. Photograph © 2000 Museum of Fine Arts, Boston. All rights reserved.

CONTENTS

4 Introduction
12 Archaeology

15 GREEK ART: AN OVERVIEW
16 Gods and Goddesses
18 Three Greek Myths
22 Heroes and Legends

23 GREEK VASES
24 Clay: All You Knead to Know
25 Black-Figure Vases
26 Red-Figure Vases
28 Graffiti and Signatures

31 GREEK SCULPTURE AND ARCHITECTURE
31 Early Greek, or Archaic, Sculpture
32 Classical Greek Sculpture
33 Hellenistic Sculpture
34 Temples

36 LIFE IN ANCIENT GREECE
36 Food, Wine, and Celebration
39 Sports and Games
42 Ancient Coins
42 Boot Camp: Preparing for War
43 Greek Art in Our Time

44 THE CLASSICAL CONNECTION

46 ROMAN ART: AN OVERVIEW
47 Pre-Roman, or Etruscan, Art

49 ROMAN SCULPTURE AND ARCHITECTURE
49 Roman Portrait Sculpture
57 Roman Architecture

62 LIFE IN ANCIENT ROME
62 Mosaics
63 Coins in Roman Art
64 Roman Legacy

65 Activities
69 Credits
71 Index

INTRODUCTION

Museum is a word like eggplant. It doesn't sound appealing. Children and adults often don't want to go to museums. How many times have you or a friend gone to a museum in anticipation of a stimulating experience? It sounds easy enough: centuries of a culture will speak to you from age-darkened canvases, sculptures, and small coins. History will come clear. Well, if history doesn't come clear, at least you'll be surrounded by many beautiful old things. Wrong!

Welcome to "museum feet."
"Museum feet" is that tired feeling you get after spending too much time in a museum. A case of "museum feet" makes you feel like saying: "This is boring. I could have done that myself. That's ugly. I'm hungry. I'm really hot. When can we sit down? What time is it?"

Word Wizard

Museum The word *museum* comes from the Greek word, *mouseion*. It means "a temple to the Muses." In Greek mythology, Zeus, king of the Greek gods, had nine beautiful daughters who never grew old. They were called the Muses and inspired creativity. Ancient Greek artists and writers asked the Muses to inspire them before they started work. We hope that you will look to a museum for inspiration, too!

Studies of museum behavior show that the average visitor spends four seconds looking at an object. Children are more interested in smells, sounds, the "feel" of a place, and other people's faces than they are in looking at a work of art. Adults, sometimes unfamiliar with what they are seeing, cannot always answer children's questions. After a museum visit, it is only a short time before most everything is forgotten. Within a family or group of five, no one member will remember a shared looking experience the same way.

We have written this book to help people of all ages enjoy new ways of looking at works of art, ways which make looking memorable and fun. Come with us and learn how to banish the **boring** and feature the **fun**.

Why *do* museums show so much old stuff? Not all museums collect old things. There are hundreds of different kinds of museums in the United States. They range from a nut museum, to a Mack truck museum, to the world's biggest thermometer museum. There is even a museum of Bad Art!

Symbols to Help You Read This Book

Use your flashlight

Common questions

A good idea

Look closely at museum objects

Additional information

Avoiding Museum Feet

To avoid museum feet, try not to look at too many things. Studies show that young visitors get more out of a visit if they focus on seven (plus or minus two) objects—either five or nine objects. The fewer objects you see, the more you'll remember. One and a half hours is the ideal time to keep your eyes and mind sharp, and your feet happy!

Making personal connections with museum objects helps to form lasting memories. For example, if you are looking at a fifteen-pound Greek marble discus, you can relate the distant past to the present by saying, "Throwing that would be like tossing four pumpkins at the same time."

"You can enjoy a work of art for as long as it takes to smell an orange. Then, to keep your interest, you have to do something more."
—SIR KENNETH CLARK,
BRITISH ART HISTORIAN, 1903–1983

This book is about doing something more.

What to bring
- ✓ Paper and pencil with eraser
- ✓ Sit-on-the-floor clothes
- ✓ A plan of action
- ✓ A small flashlight
- ✓ A snack for the ride

Finding Your Way

A museum may feel big and confusing when you first arrive. If you are not familiar with the museum, find the Information Center or a guard. Ask for directions to the collection that you want to see. Rooms in a museum are called **galleries.** Museums are not the only places that have galleries. Prairie dogs, moles, and ants live in underground galleries. Old ships had galleries and so did forts.

What do BC and AD mean after dates? In 532 AD, a monk named Dennis the Short came up with a system to date events in history. He chose the year he believed Christ was born and called it 1 AD, Anno Domini, Latin for *the year of our Lord.* Everything that happened after Christ's birth is identified by the letters AD. Events that occurred before Christ's birth are identified by the letters BC, which stand for *before Christ.* The year 50 BC is farther away in time than 10 BC.

Instruments/thingamabobs in museum galleries and cases

Some visitors are as interested in conservation equipment as they are in the objects on display. The *hygrometer* is a small dial that measures the humidity inside a display case. The *hygrothermograph* is a larger device that records the temperature and humidity of a museum gallery. These are often seen on the floor in a corner of the gallery. *Silica gel* are small crystals that control humidity change in exhibit cases.

Why can't we touch things? Fingers contain grease and acid which hurt fragile museum objects. Have you ever seen the mark your fingerprint leaves on a blackboard?

"God housekeeping" Periodically, members of a museum's conservation department may visit gods, emperors, and other objects in the Greek and Roman collection for a dusting. Using a soft brush, they direct the dust toward a small, powerful vacuum cleaner that is equipped with a HEPA filter. (HEPA means high-efficiency particle-arresting.) The vacuum cleaner never touches the sculpture. It sucks up the dust and traps it inside a sealed bag.

Did you Know...

Labels

Every work of art in a museum has a label. In a Greek collection, a label might look like this.

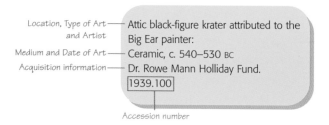

Location, Type of Art and Artist — Attic black-figure krater attributed to the Big Ear painter:

Medium and Date of Art — Ceramic, c. 540–530 BC

Acquisition information — Dr. Rowe Mann Holliday Fund.

1939.100

Accession number

Let's look at the label above. You are looking at a *krater*, which is a vase or container used for mixing wine and water. "Attic" means it came from Athens, not the top floor of a house. It is decorated in the black-figure style of vase painting. While the artist did not sign this vase, scholars recognize it as the work of an artist they called the Big Ear painter. The figures in his work always have big ears! Dr. Rowe Mann Holliday gave money to the museum to be used for purchasing art.

Accession Numbers   Museums keep track of their collections by assigning a number, called the accession number, to each object they own. The accession number on the label is 1939.100. This indicates that the museum acquired the krater in 1939. It was the hundredth object to come into the museum that year. Sometimes, if you look carefully, you can spot accession numbers written on the back or side of museum objects.

Your Turn to Smell the Orange

Now it is *your* turn to smell the orange. That's what we call getting your first impression. Choose an object. Let your eyes wander all over the surface. Absorb it. It is special, and it is yours. If you are looking at a sculpture, walk all around it if you can.

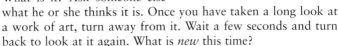

Look at it face to face, from its side and its back. Squat down and look up. Taking time to look at a work of art is important because there is usually more to a work of art than first meets the eye.

Study this drawing carefully. What is it? Ask someone else what he or she thinks it is. Once you have taken a long look at a work of art, turn away from it. Wait a few seconds and turn back to look at it again. What is *new* this time?

Look at Color

Colors can make us feel a certain way. They send messages. There are warm and cool colors. Warm colors are reds, oranges, and yellows. They might make us think of fire. Restaurant owners often use red in their decor because it can make people feel hungry. Cool colors are blues, greens, and violets. They might make us think of glaciers and ice. Rooms in hot climates are often painted blue to look cool and fresh.

Think about what different colors mean to you. Is yellow a cheerful color? Does it make you think of sunshine? Vincent van Gogh, the Dutch artist, said that for him yellow was the color of love. Does black seem scary or sad? Does it bring to mind being alone in a dark house at night? Endless space?

Originally, Greek and Roman stone sculptures were at least partly painted. Eyes, hair, and clothing were brightly colored. Women's flesh was often left unpainted, but men's flesh was sometimes tinted pale brown. Limestone, less beautiful than marble, was usually painted. Red, blue, and yellow were the most commonly used colors, but green, black, and brown were popular, too.

Peplos Kore, ca. 6th century BC.

Temples like the Parthenon were also partly painted. Paint was applied to temple sculptures and to the backgrounds of pediments and friezes. Columns were sometimes tinted to reduce the sun's glare, but the capitals were normally left bare. Early Roman temples had painted decoration, too.

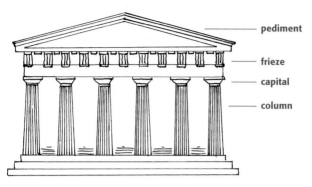

- pediment
- frieze
- capital
- column

Look at Shape

You can find lots of shapes in Greek vase painting. Early vases were painted in a geometric style. The vases are divided into bands and decorated with shapes you'll recognize: triangles, concentric circles, semicircles, and diamonds.

Another common shape in Greek art is the scroll, or *volute*. It has been suggested that the Greeks liked this shape because it reminded them of ocean waves. The top (capital) of an Ionic column is decorated with hanging scrolls. Look for scroll shapes on Greek and Roman column capitals.

Oinochoe, 8th century BC.

Ionic capital with hanging scrolls.

Look at Line

Lines can be diagonal, curved, vertical, and horizontal. Diagonal lines are action lines. Curved lines also lend a sense of motion. A vertical line is a strong, stable line. It gives a feeling of balance. A horizontal line is a quiet line.

Word Wizard

Horizontal The word *horizontal* comes from *horizon,* the seemingly flat line where the earth meets the sky.

One of the most characteristic lines in ancient Greek art is the *meander,* or Greek key pattern. Horizontal and vertical at the same time, the meander is one continuous line that keeps turning at right angles to make a geometric pattern that looks like the repetition of the shape of an old key.

Word Wizard

Meander is the name of a river in Greece. The word *meander* means to wander, like a river, on a winding path.

Look at Composition

The way an artist arranges the color, line, and shape in a work of art is called composition. When you decorate a birthday cake or doodle on a frosty windowpane, you are making a composition. Artists plan their compositions to guide our eyes on a journey through their artwork.

Greek vase painters were not interested in creating perspective. They arranged their designs to exist on the surface only. Decoration is divided into horizontal zones or registers. Forms are flat. Sometimes, distant figures were painted higher than others to create a sense of space. The Romans, however, created space in their wall paintings with architectural motifs and vanishing points that lead our eyes into a composition.

Exekias, *Amphora,* black-figure vase. Find horizontal registers showing horses being harnessed, lions, and boars.

Look at Sculpture

A sculpture is an object that can be measured three ways. It has length, width, and thickness or a front, a back, and sides—three dimensions. Since earliest times, people have made sculptures out of clay, bone, wood, and stone. Some sculptures are created by *carving away* material, like a pumpkin. In others, you *add* materials as you do when you make a snowman or a drip sandcastle. They can be huge like the Sphinx or tiny like a Stone Age arrowhead.

Today, there are very few free-standing ancient Greek sculptures left in the world, but there are thousands of Roman copies. Bronze was the most popular material for sculpture in ancient Greece and Rome, but most bronze pieces were melted down for other uses in times of emergency. Stone sculptures, too, were often thrown into lime-burning kilns or broken up to be used in walls or foundations of buildings. Sculptures also fell prey to thieves, earthquakes, and fire. Most Greek and Roman sculptures in today's museums were carved from limestone or marble.

Charioteer of Delphi. This life-size fifth-century bronze sculpture was excavated from Delphi where an earthquake had buried it. It shows what the many bronze statues lost to us today might have looked like. Remains of four bronze horses and a chariot were found next to it. This bronze sculpture owes its survival to the earthquake that buried it.

ARCHAEOLOGY

The word **archaeology** comes from two Greek words: *archaia* meaning "old" and *logos* meaning "science." Archaeology is the study of old things. Archaeologists are detectives. Each object they find is a clue to how people lived thousands of years ago. Almost everything we know about ancient Greece is a result of the work of archaeologists.

Can you think of other words that end in *-ology*? Zoology is the study of animals. Gemology is the study of precious stones or gems. What is mythology?

Giant of Greek Archaeology: Heinrich Schliemann German archaeologist Heinrich Schliemann (1822–1890) worked as a grocery clerk selling whiskey and herring before founding a successful import firm. In 1866, he quit to follow his childhood dream of excavating Troy.

Did You Know...

Schliemann wrote that this picture in the *Children's History of the World*, caught his imagination and inspired him to excavate the city of Troy.

Some children decide at an early age what they want to be when they grow up. When Heinrich Schliemann was seven, he told his father, "When I am big I shall go...and find Troy and the King's treasure." He claims he became "hooked" by a picture of Troy burning in a book his father had given him for Christmas. When he became an archaeologist, he studied Homer's *Iliad* for clues to Troy's location. He chose to start digging near "two fair-flowing springs, where two fountains rise."

Seven years later, when he was peering down into his excavation pit, he spotted the glint of gold. Afraid that his workers might steal it, he ordered them to take a break. When they left, he dug out a helmet and a silver vase with nine thousand gold objects inside! Schliemann donated much of his Trojan treasure to the German Museum of Ethnology.

ART OOPS!

Fact or fiction? Scholars suspect that Schliemann did not find all the Trojan gold in one place. They think he saved objects from many levels of the excavation and put them all together to form an artificial "King's Treasure."

GOLD AT RUSH HOUR The largest excavation ever to take place in Greece was the 1998 dig for an eleven-mile subway system in Athens. Three hundred archaeologists have found a bathhouse, ancient roads, coins, black-figure vases, and gold jewelry.

ART SCOOP

Snakes alive! Working on an archaeological dig sounds exciting. What fun it would be to scoop up clumps of dirt, each promising the sparkle of a jewel or gold. Schliemann's excavation journals, however, hint at the other side of the story. Alarming inconveniences to his dig at Troy were snakes, scorpions, and a centipede called *Saranto-podia* ("forty footer"), which was rumored to have a fatal bite. Snakes aside, archaeologists also often contend with searing sun, high winds, and aching backs. Artifacts are painstakingly unearthed at a snail's pace with picks, trowels, and even brushes. And, after all that, mostly what they find is broken pottery, called potsherds. Jewels are very few and far between.

Sophie Schliemann, ca. 1892. Schliemann's wife, Sophia, models some of the gold treasure horde found at Troy.

FEAT OF CLAY! A fired clay pot is fragile, but pieces of broken pottery are almost impossible to destroy. Once clay is fired in a kiln, it becomes resistant to water, salts, gases, and acids. Since it was both common and durable, you might say clay was the plastic of the ancient world. Potsherds provide some of the oldest clues to how ancient people lived.

Did You Know...

Years ago, people could take archaeological remains from foreign countries. Records were not kept. The sculptured friezes from the Greek Parthenon, now in the British Museum, were taken to England in 1806. Many objects in museums today were removed from foreign countries by travelers and collectors before it was against the law to do so.

Today, an archaeologist must receive a contract to dig in a foreign country. Every object that is discovered belongs to the country where it is found. The local government gets first pick from the dig and decides what the archaeologist may keep.

Archaeologist excavating in Greece.

Word Wizard

Artifact The word *artifact* is an archaeological term for something dug up. It comes from the Latin, *arte,* meaning "art," and *factum,* meaning "something made."

How do things get buried? Leaves, animals, dust in the atmosphere, sand, construction, and earthworms can help cover things up. Earthworms cause particular problems for archaeologists because they mix up layers of soil used in dating. This disturbance of the soil is called **bioturbation.**

GREEK ART: AN OVERVIEW

The beauty and enduring influence of Greek art disguises the fact that only a small part of what once existed can be seen in museums today. Classical bronze sculptures were scrapped or melted down for their metal in later times of economic downturn and war. Greek painting has vanished over the centuries. Even stone sculpture has succumbed to the ravages of time, looting, and natural disasters. Greek temples survive, in part, but cannot be transported to museums. Thus, museums must convey the importance of Greek architecture with scale models and photographs of existing ruins. Thanks to Etruscan burial practices, however, many Greek vases were preserved in central Italian tombs. Greek vases can be seen in many museums. In addition, some museums show paintings of Greek gods and mythology in their European art collections.

George F. Watts, *The Minotaur,* 1885. Angry that King Minos of Crete did not honor him with the sacrifice of a snow white bull, Poseidon, god of the sea, arranged for the birth of a monster called the Minotaur. The Minotaur, a man with a bull's head, ravaged Crete until it was locked up in a labyrinth where it waited to devour an annual tribute of fourteen youths and maidens from Athens.

The Bare Facts About Greek Art

First-time museum viewers may be surprised to find that most sculptures of Greek gods, heroes, and athletes are shown without clothes. This is because the Greeks were the first people to discover how to realistically portray and even "improve" the human body in art—giving it beautifully proportioned limbs, well-developed muscles, and idealized contours. What better way to honor gods and heroes than to show them in their perfect natural form? Covering the body with clothes only concealed its natural beauty. For this reason, Greek society accepted nudity. Athletes practiced and competed in the nude, and countless statues honoring them were placed in public spaces.

The ancient Greeks worshiped many gods, but the twelve gods who lived on Mt. Olympus and belonged to the family of Zeus were the most important. The Greeks assumed that the gods acted and looked like humans, except they didn't get sick or die. The gods could be jealous and scheming, but each one controlled an important part of human life. The Greeks found many ways to please their gods. They worshiped them in sanctuaries, held festivals in their honor, sacrificed animals to them at open-air altars, and dedicated statues and magnificent temples to them. Identifying gods and goddesses in museum art is a bit like bird watching. All the gods have their own "field marks." The easiest place to find the Greek gods in a museum is on Greek vases. While myths portray the gods as a quarrelsome family, they are calm and dignified in Greek art.

Head of Homer. The sunken eyes in this portrait suggest the poet's legendary blindness.

HOMER: HE, SHE, OR THEY?

It is widely accepted that Homer, a ninth to eighth-century BC poet, first named and described the duties of the major Greek gods in his book, the *Iliad*. But the man himself is a mystery. Some scholars even debate whether Homer really existed. Many believe that the *Iliad* was a series of tales passed down by word of mouth from minstrel to minstrel. One expert argues that Homer was a woman.

APHRODITE
Goddess of love and beauty, Aphrodite is married to the lame blacksmith god, Hephaistus, but prefers Ares. In Greek art, she is often shown with her winged son, Eros. Occasionally Aphrodite holds a mirror.

Myth Mate: The Roman goddess of love and beauty is called **Venus.** Her son is called Cupid.

APOLLO
God of light and music. In art, he holds a lyre, a laurel, or a bow. The Romans did not rename Apollo.

MT. OLYMPUS

The highest mountain in Greece was home to the twelve major gods in Greek mythology. Its frequent cloud cover made it mysterious and hid godly machinations from human eyes.

Mt. Olympus. This 9,573-foot mountain in northern Greece is a popular climb for hikers today.

ARES   God of war and Aphrodite's lover. In art, he wears a helmet and armor and holds a shield and spear.

Myth Mate: The Roman god of war is called Mars. Since he represented the conquering spirit of the Roman empire, Mars was important in Roman art.

ARTEMIS   Goddess of the hunt, wild animals, and child-birth. Artemis is the twin sister of Apollo. In art, she holds a bow and arrow, and is sometimes accompanied by a deer.

Myth Mate: The Roman counterpart to Artemis is **Diana.**

ATHENA   Zeus' favorite daughter is the goddess of wisdom, arts and crafts, and war, as well as being the patron goddess of Athens. In art, she holds a spear or shield and wears an *aegis* (breastplate) decorated with a Gorgon's head. She usually wears a helmet.

Myth Mate: The Roman goddess of wisdom is called **Minerva.**

DEMETER   Goddess of agriculture and sister of Zeus. In art, Demeter's symbol is a torch or an ear of corn.

Myth Mate: The Roman goddess of crops and harvest is called **Ceres.**

Word Wizard

Our word **cereal** comes from Ceres' association with grain.

HERA   Goddess of marriage and the jealous wife of Zeus. In art, she sometimes wears a crown or carries a scepter. In myths, she spends time taking revenge on the women with whom Zeus has fallen in love.

Myth Mate: The Roman goddess of household and marriage is called **Juno.**

HERMES
A son of Zeus, Hermes is the messenger god. He is also a god of travelers and trade. In art, he wears a wide-brimmed hat *(petasos)* and winged sandals. He holds a *caduceus* (snakes wrapped around a magic winged staff) which he uses to guide souls to the underworld.

Myth Mate: The Roman messenger god is called **Mercury.** In Roman art, Mercury sometimes carries a purse in his right hand because he was associated with commerce and gold coins.

PERSEPHONE
Persephone is shown in Greek art with a pomegranate symbol or an ear of corn.

Myth Mate: Persephone's Roman counterpart is called **Proserpine.**

ZEUS
King of the gods and associated with thunder and lightning. In art, Zeus is bearded. Sometimes he sits on a throne holding thunderbolts. He falls in love easily. When he does, he hides himself in a big, fluffy cloud so his wife, Hera, won't see him. Myths say he was born in a cave on Crete and fed honey by bumblebees and milk by a goat.

Myth Mate: The Roman king of the gods is called **Jupiter.**

Three Greek Myths

The Judgment of Paris

At a wedding on Mount Olympus, an uninvited guest, Eris, goddess of strife, threw a golden apple marked "for the fairest" in front of Zeus. The contestants were Hera, Aphrodite, and Athena. Afraid of insulting any of the three goddesses by picking only one to receive the apple, Zeus asked the Trojan shepherd Paris to choose for him. Hera offered Paris power if he chose her, Athena offered victory in battle, and Aphrodite offered herself as the most beautiful woman in the world. Paris chose Aphrodite.

Neck Amphora, ca. 525 BC. Antimenes Painter, Black-figure vase.
The scene on this Greek amphora shows Hermes leading Hera, Athena, and Aphrodite to the judgment of Paris.

The Birth of Athena from Zeus' Forehead

When he heard that a goddess named Metis would bear a child who would overthrow him, Zeus swallowed her. He got a terrible headache, and Athena was born, fully armed, from his forehead.

Black-figured Amphora, Birth of Athena, ca. 540 BC.

A   Closer Look

• In *The Birth of Athena,* find Hermes' caduceus, sun hat, and winged boots; Zeus' thunderbolts, and Ares' armor. Notice Zeus' toes, too!
• Find Athena's shield, spear, and helmet.

■ Can you find three symbols that identify Hermes?
■ Look for Hera and Athena. How can you identify them?

Every time I hear a myth it's different. Why? Several writers in ancient times recorded different versions of Greek myths. Homer was the first to describe the family of twelve Greek gods. Another poet, Hesiod (700s BC), and the Roman poet Ovid (43 BC–17 AD), wrote their own accounts of the myths and legends of ancient Greece.

The Abduction of Persephone by Hades

Persephone, daughter of Demeter, goddess of agriculture, was picking flowers when Hades, king of the Underworld, spotted her and carried her down to his kingdom. In Hades, she ate some pomegranate seeds from Hades' forbidden garden. This offense forced her to live in the underworld for half of each year. Every year, Demeter grieved while Persephone was gone, causing winter to grip the earth. When Persephone returned, Demeter's joy brought the warmth of spring and the summer's harvest.

Christophe Schwarz, *The Abduction of Persephone*, ca. 1570.

IT'S ALL GREEK TO ME!

Write a word in Greek letters using this chart:

Α	Β	Γ	Δ	Ε	Ζ	Η	Θ	Ι	Κ	Λ	Μ
A	B	G	D	E	Z	E	TH	I	K	L	M

Ν	Ξ	Ο	Π	Ρ	Σ	Τ	Υ	Φ	Ψ	Χ	Ω
N	X	O	P	R	S	T	Y/U	PH	PS	CH	O

Raising Hades

Wasn't Hades a place, too? Yes. Hades' Underworld kingdom was called Hades. *Hades* means "unseen." The ancient Greeks believed that the spirits of the dead, called *shades*, went to live in this dismal, chilly place. Cerberus—a three-headed dog who wagged his tail for newcomers and gobbled up those who tried to escape—guarded Hades.

Myth Mate: The Roman god of the underworld is called **Pluto.**

Did only bad people go to Hades? The Greeks believed that almost everyone went to Hades. It was a dismal place, but not a place of punishment. Only saintly people and heroes went to the Elysian Fields, a paradise of warm breezes at the end of the earth.

ONE-WAY TICKET TO HADES, PLEASE. Some bodies buried under grave-marker vases (called *Dipylon* vases) have been found with coins under their tongues. The money was to pay Charon, the mythological boatman who ferried their spirits across the river to Hades.

Jon Roddam Spencer-Stanhope, *Psyche and Charon.* Charon is taking a "fare" from Psyche's mouth. "Shades" of the dead are in the background.

Greek painters decorated their vases with legends about their heroes. In their legends, a Greek hero was usually the offspring of a god or king. Think of them as ancient Supermen.

Herakles
Herakles was the most popular hero in Greek art and a son of Zeus. His stepmother, Hera, despised him and sent him a spell, which made him kill his children. Herakles was told he could make up for his crime by doing twelve labors. The labors included killing the Nemean lion, capturing a golden horned stag, and delivering Cerberus, the three-headed guard dog of Hades, to earth. In art, Herakles wears a lion skin around his neck and a lion mask on his head.

Plate: *Herakles, Hermes, & Cerberus,* ca. 520 BC.

A modern model in Hissarlik (modern Troy) shows what the wooden horse might have looked like.

The Trojan War
This legendary war started when the Trojan prince, Paris, kidnapped Helen of Greece, the most beautiful woman in the world. Greek soldiers sailed after her to Troy but could not enter the city gates. To trick the Trojans into opening the gates, several soldiers hid in a huge wooden horse outside the city. Believing it was a gift from the gods, the Trojans brought the horse into the city. After dark, the Greek soldiers swarmed out of the horse and opened the gates to the Greek army. After a terrible battle, the Greeks sacked Troy and headed home with Helen. Homer's poem, *The Iliad,* describes the last days of the Trojan War.

GREEK VASES

Terra-cotta vases form a large part of any museum collection of Greek art. Although they are called vases, the ancient Greeks did not use them for decoration or to hold flowers. Instead, each type of vase had a specific purpose. There were four general categories of use: storage, mixing, pouring, and drinking. The painted scenes on Greek vases tell us about daily life and Greek mythology.

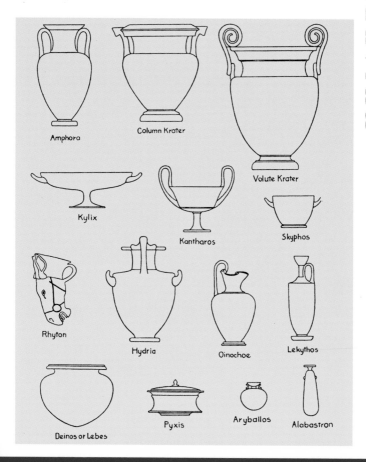

Amphora

Column Krater

Volute Krater

Kylix

Kantharos

Skyphos

Rhyton

Hydria

Oinochoe

Lekythos

Deinos or Lebes

Pyxis

Aryballos

Alabastron

Going to pot! Describing a Greek vase can be like describing a person. Both have lips, necks, shoulders, bellies, and even feet. Even experts use these terms to describe parts of a vase. Amphoras, kraters, drinking cups, and hydrias are the most common vase shapes. Many people just call Greek vases pots!

Word Wizard

Hydria A Greek hydria was used to hold water. It had three handles; two to hold while lifting and one to hold while pouring. *Hydria* is the Greek word for water. How many other "water" words can you think of? Hydrant? Dehydration? Hydrangea?

MOUTH
NECK
SHOULDER
BELLY
FOOT

Clay: All You Knead to Know

What is terra cotta? Unglazed baked clay is called terra cotta. It means "baked earth" in Italian. In ancient Greece and Rome, it was used for vases, sculpture, and building decoration.

How were pots shaped? Since 1,000 BC, Greek pots were shaped on a potter's wheel. Small pots were made in one piece; larger pots in sections. Handmade handles were added separately. When the vase was bone-dry, it was placed in a wood-fueled kiln and fired at 950 degrees centigrade (1,742 degrees fahrenheit).

What makes Greek pots that orange-red color? The clay around Athens had a high iron content. When it was fired in a kiln, the iron turned the clay a reddish color.

Did Greek vases cost much when they were made? They cost between one and three days' wages! But that was then! Now a signed Greek vase in mint condition might be worth over one million dollars.

Black-Figure Vases

The earliest type of Greek vase painting started around 700 BC and was called black-figure painting. When the clay was "leather hard," figures and motifs were painted in black silhouette using a creamy mixture of clay and water called "slip." Details, such as clothing and faces, were incised, or scratched, into the slip before firing. Other colors were sometimes added: white for women's skin; red for hair, horse manes, and clothing details. The slip turned black after firing while the background and incised details remained the natural color of the clay.

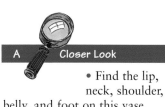

A Closer Look

- Find the lip, neck, shoulder, belly, and foot on this vase.
- What color are the figures? Their arms? Their hair?
- What color is the background of the vase?
- Can you find an amphora with a lid in your museum?

Herakles and Boar. Black-figure vase.

THE ALL-PURPOSE AMPHORA Amphoras were used for storing grain, oil, or wine. They have two handles to grip when carrying them. Some amphoras still bear traces of ancient wine. Amphoras were made with lids, but most are now lost.

What is a silhouette? It is an outline image, filled in with black. Named for French King Louis XV's cost-cutting minister of finance, Etienne de Silhouette (1709–1767) silhouettes were originally black-paper cutouts of people's profiles—inexpensive stand-ins for a portrait.

Red-Figure Vases

Red-figure vase painting started later than black-figure, around 530 BC. The red-figure style was the reverse of black-figure painting. Black "slip" was used to paint the background only. Figures remained the natural clay color. The advantage of red-figure painting was that the artist could use the varied thickness of a brush line to show muscles, facial features, and body contours. The brush gave the design a more fluid feel than a scratched line could. Red-figure painting eventually replaced almost all black-figure painting.

Red-figure vase. ca. 450-440 BC.

- What color are the figures on the above vase? The background?
- Can you find other red-figure vases in your museum?
- Can you find a black-figure vase?

A   Closer Look

Tempest in a Greek pot During a visit to an American museum, a German archaeologist noticed that a seventh-century BC Greek vase was missing a piece. By chance, he happened to know that the missing piece was in Germany! The German museum offered the piece to the American museum so that the vase could be displayed whole. Since it was illegal for the German museum to give away any artwork, the piece was loaned long-term instead.

Repairing potholes Why don't museums hide ugly cracks and repair holes in their pots? Today's conservators make their repairs reversible in case a new piece of information is discovered and a repair needs to be changed. Pots are mended with a glue that can be loosened later without hurting the object. Disguising cracks or filling holes would make it harder to take the vase apart for repairs!

WHITE-GROUND VASES

White-ground vases are less common than black- and red-figure vases in Greek art. They are painted with a white "slip." The most common type of white-ground vase is called a *lekythos*. The lekythos held oils used in funeral rites. Scenes on a lekythos often relate to rituals surrounding death.

Women Bearing Grave Offering, ca. 450–420 BC. White-ground lekythos.

A **Closer Look**

• What is the scene on the lekythos? (A woman is bringing a perfume jar as a tomb offering.)
• What colors are used on this vase?
• Find a white-ground vase in your museum.

A helpful vase
These wine cups have a huge pair of eyes painted on one side. Drinkers may have thought the eyes guarded them when the cup blocked their view.

Kylix Attic Black-figure Eye Cup, ca. 520–500 BC. When this cup is tipped to the mouth, it looks like a big-eyed mask with its foot acting as the mouth and its handles as the ears.

Eye jinx There is still superstition about eyes today in Greece. Many people keep a blue glass "evil eye" charm to ward off bad luck.

Did you know...

Graffiti and Signatures

Signatures
Few ancient Greek artists signed their vases. Sometimes, however, one wrote "So-and-so *epoisen* (ancient Greek for "made") or "So-and-so *egraphsen*," (ancient Greek for "painted"). Even

without a signature, scholars can often recognize artists by their style. For example, one Greek artist is known as the "elbows-out" painter, because of the way his figures are depicted.

Polite pots Sometimes a pot will bear a message that says, "I greet you."

Passionate pots Some pots have "love inscriptions" that say, "So-and-so is beautiful." It was common to find names of well-known Athenian athletes on Greek pots. A love inscription on a Greek vase will look like this:

"Ajax *kalos.*" ("Ajax is beautiful.")

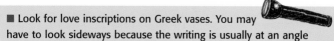

- Look for love inscriptions on Greek vases. You may have to look sideways because the writing is usually at an angle
- Look for the words *epoisen* or *egraphsen*.
- Find a pot with a distinct feature that would give the artist a name. What name comes to mind?
- Look for signs of a repair on a vase.

Designs and Patterns

Greek vase painters used different borders and motifs to decorate their pots, frame scenes, and fill space. The following, which also appear on architecture, are among the most common patterns.

Acanthus A plant with prickly, spiky leaves.

Dentil Think dentist! This pattern looks like teeth.

Greek key, or meander, design This design often wraps around a Greek vase.

Lotus and Palmette leaves Lotus and palm leaves that fan out.

- Locate a Greek key, or meander, design on a vase in your museum. Can you find other motifs?
- Can you find a palmette, lotus, acanthus, or dentil pattern?

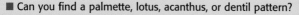

Alert! Most-Wanted Monsters

Greek myths and legends describe many gruesome monsters. They are part animal and part human or are a combination of several animals in one. Monsters may have served to explain scary natural forces such as whirlpools or earthquakes that people didn't understand. Greek vases are good places to stalk monsters in a museum.

Sphinx The ancient Greek sphinx has the body of a lion, eagle wings, and a woman's head. It was often a guardian figure. (Egyptian sphinxes are wingless and have a man's head.)

Centaur A man with the body and hind legs of a horse.

Gorgons Three sisters with glowering faces and snakes for hair. A look at them turned people to stone. Medusa was the only mortal Gorgon. In art, Gorgons have grinning faces, stuck-out tongues, snub noses, and staring eyes.

Sirens Part-woman part-bird, these creatures sang sweet songs that lured sailors to their deaths on rocky shores. According to Homer's epic poem, the *Odyssey,* Ulysses and his crew were the only men to survive their call.

Word Wizard

Siren Our word *siren* comes from the songs of Greek sirens.

A   Closer Look

• In your museum's galleries, look for centaurs, sphinxes, and Gorgon heads.
• Which monster seems the scariest? Why?

GREEK SCULPTURE AND ARCHITECTURE

The ancient Greeks were the first people to focus on making realistic images of the human form. Greek sculptors created images of gods, heroes, and athletes to place in religious sanctuaries, marketplaces, and other public locations.

? Why do so many statues have broken noses? After Christianity spread to Greece, some sculptures were defaced because they represented the "old" or pagan gods. Other sculptures' noses may have broken while being moved or during natural disasters such as earthquakes. Remember, some Greek sculptures are 2,500 years old!

Where did Greeks get marble for their statues? Most of it came from the Greek islands of Paros, Naxos, and Thasos. There were also marble quarries on Mt. Hymettos and Mt. Pentelikon on the mainland near Athens.

Early Greek, or Archaic, Sculpture

One of the earliest types of Greek sculpture is a *kouros,* a standing naked male youth. Probably influenced by Egyptian art, these figures stand stiffly facing forward with their hands at their sides and their left legs forward. Their waists are thin, and they have beaded beards and hair. Their eyes are almond-shaped, and they have a slight smile called the "archaic" smile. Kouros figures were used as grave markers or as offerings of respect to the gods. A clothed female statue of this type is called a *kore.*

What is an archaic smile? This smile is a mystery to scholars. Some think it comes from a deep undercutting of stone at the corners of the mouth. Others suggest that the smile was meant to make the statue seem more lifelike; or perhaps it was intended to express a sense of well-being. The archaic smile—present even on wounded warriors—was a feature of early Greek sculpture.

Head of a Man, 480 BC.

A   Closer Look

• Find an archaic smile and imitate it.
• Stand like an archaic kouros.
• Visit an Egyptian collection and compare an Egyptian standing figure with a Greek kouros.

Classical Greek Sculpture

The high point of Greek sculpture came after the Greek city-states defeated the Persians in the Persian Wars of 490 and 480 BC. A new sense of confidence filled the country, accompanied by economic prosperity and achievement in the arts. Classical sculptures reflected the mood of the times. In them, the human form was idealized, and expressions were calm and untroubled. The body grew more powerful and changed its stance. No longer facing forward as in the Archaic Period, classical figures turned slightly and shifted their weight to one foot. This stance is called *contrapposto*.

Polykleitos, *Doryphoros,* ca. 450–440 BC. Doryphorous means "spear bearer." This is a Roman copy, in marble, of a Greek bronze sculpture that is now lost. This statue and the original fifth-century BC bronze sculpture by Polykleitos of Argos are examples of contrapposto.

What is contrapposto? Although it sounds like Italian food, this Italian term means "to set opposite or contrast." It describes a stance in Greek art in which weight is borne on one leg while the other is relaxed. The hip of the weight-bearing leg is higher than the other hip, and the body turns slightly. Contrapposto is also known as the "Grecian slump."

What does Classical mean? It means the highest standard. Qualities of classical art are simplicity, proportion, and harmony.

A Closer Look

• Try standing contrapposto, like the Doryphoros.
• What words describe the expression on the spear bearer's face?
• Find other contrapposto sculptures in your museum.

Hellenistic Sculpture

By 348 BC, Alexander the Great had conquered Greece and much of the Mediterranean. A larger empire of many cultures brought changes in Greek sculpture. The ideal, serene figures of classical Greece became more animated. Faces showed emotion, and the human form began to bend, twist, and turn in its space. Portraits became more individualized, showing a variety of everyday subjects from old and deformed people to fishermen and peasants. Hellenistic means Greek-like, and derives from the word *Hellene,* which refers to a native of Greece.

Wrestlers, late 2nd century BC.

A Closer Look

• Compare the wrestlers with an archaic Greek kouros.
• Look for Hellenistic sculpture. Imitate a face or body movement.

Beginning in the seventh century BC, the ancient Greeks built temples to honor their gods. Outside, these sacred buildings were supported by fluted columns (with vertical grooves) and adorned with painted sculptures. Inside, they housed statues of gods and goddesses. One of the most beautiful temples from ancient Greece is the Parthenon (completed 438 BC). Standing on Athens' Acropolis, or "high place," the Parthenon was built in honor of Athena, the patron goddess of Athens. Symbols of grace and stability, Greek temples have been widely copied and admired.

Parthenon, 448–432 BC. Architects Ictinus and Callicrates designed this Doric-style temple. It originally housed a colossal statue of the goddess Athena made of ivory and gold.

ART SCOOP

Plundered or preserved? By 1800, most sculpture on the west side of the Parthenon had been destroyed or stolen. Lord Elgin (English ambassador to Turkish-controlled Greece) asked to remove the remaining sculpture for safekeeping. He was granted a license by the Turkish government and later donated the sculptures to the British Museum. Though the British government had promised to reimburse him for half the cost of shipping the sculptures back to England, he was never fully repaid. Elgin was in debt for the rest of his life. The "Elgin Marbles" are still in the British Museum, and the British government has supplied copies of the sculptures to replace the originals on the Parthenon.

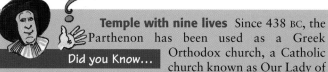
Out of bounds Because of their fragile antiquities, Athens and Rome were declared **"open cities"** during World War II. An "open city" cannot be attacked or fortified during a war.

The Three Orders

The three orders, or styles, of Greek temple architecture are Doric, Ionic, and Corinthian. The difference between orders is most easily seen in the column capitals (the top part of columns).

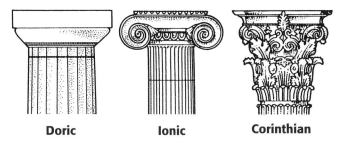

Doric   **Ionic**   **Corinthian**

Doric The Doric column is the oldest and simplest Greek column. It has a fluted shaft and a square block as its capital.

Ionic The Ionic column has a fluted shaft and a pair of volutes (scrolls) on its capital front and back.

Corinthian The Corinthian column has volutes (scrolls) that spring from rows of acanthus leaves.

A   Closer Look

• Look at buildings in your hometown for Ionic, Doric, and Corinthian columns.
• Look at the back of a penny and a nickel. What kind of columns do you see? (Doric)

Food, Wine, and Celebration

Parties known as *symposia* were an important part of upper-class life in ancient Greece. Symposia took place in the men's quarters of private homes. Servants and entertainers were the only women allowed. Guests wore garlands on their head and reclined on couches along the sides of the room. Speeches, riddles, poetry, and music were part of the entertainment. At the end of the evening, guests might play a game called *cottabos* (wine throw) to see who could use their last drops of wine to hit or sink targets floating in water. Scenes of symposia are commonly painted on Greek drinking cups.

Kylix, ca. 480 BC., detail. Attributed to Foundry painter, Athens. This red-figure scene shows a man and a youth on a couch, playing cottabos.

A   Closer Look

• Notice the guest reclining on a sofa for two. What is he about to do with his right hand? (play cottabos with his drinking cup)
• Is this a red- or a black-figure scene?
• Notice the garlands on the figures' heads.

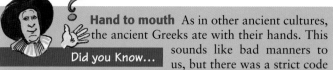

Hand to mouth As in other ancient cultures, the ancient Greeks ate with their hands. This sounds like bad manners to us, but there was a strict code for eating. Bread was eaten with the left hand only. The right hand brought all other food to the mouth. Diners leaned back and propped themselves up on their left elbows.

Did you Know...

DIONYSUS The most commonly shown god in ancient Greek art, Dionysus was the god of wine and fertility. In myths, Dionysus was born from Zeus' thigh. In art, Dionysus is bearded and usually naked. He wears a crown of grape leaves and often holds a wine cup. Sometimes he holds a wand with a pine cone tip, called a *thyrsus*. He is usually attended by *maenads* (women followers who carry musical instruments) and satyrs who have tails, snub noses, beards, and goats' cloven hoofs.

Myth Mate: The Roman god of wine and theater was **Bacchus.**

Kantharos, or drinking cups *Kantharos* have large handles. The handles were used to hang the cups on wall pegs.

A GRAPE STORY Wine was the everyday drink of people of all classes in ancient Greece and Rome. Wine was diluted with water and strained before serving.

Krater This large vase was used for mixing wine with water. At parties, it was placed in the middle of the room so the guests could enjoy its design. The ideal number of kraters to be used at a symposium, or party, was three.

Word Wizard

Krater The Greek word *krater* has given us our word *crater,* which we use to describe the center of a volcano. Can you see how a krater and a crater are alike?

Oinochoe (pronounced *oh knock away*) Slaves dipped this serving pitcher into a wine-filled krater and then poured wine into guests' cups.

• Notice the kantharos which Dionysus holds and the grapes around him. Find his crown of grape leaves.
• Find a satyr.
• With a magnifying glass, find Dionysus' name above his head.
• Find a drinking cup in your gallery. What scenes are painted on it?
• Find an oinochoai to dip into a krater.

Amphora, ca. 540 BC. This black-figure vase shows Dionysus drinking wine in a grape arbor.

A woman's place Women stayed home in ancient Greece. Their job was to run the household, bring up the children, and spin and weave in their separate quarters in the back of the house. Greek women made their own clothes. Wealthy women only left home to go to funerals, weddings, and religious occasions. In Greek vase painting, you find women getting married, doing household chores, getting water from the fountain house, and in various other scenes with their servants.

All the Fashion In early times, women wore a *peplos,* which was a long tunic made from a square piece of material (like a sleeveless nightgown), and sandals. A peplos was pinned together at the shoulders with a *fibula,* or safety pin, and sometimes it was worn with a

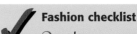

Fashion checklist
○ peplos
○ himation
○ chiton
○ fibula
○ hairnet or ribbon

cloak called a *himation.* In later times, Greek women wore a *chiton,* which was like a peplos with sleeves. In Greek vase painting, women have whitish skin and almond-shaped eyes. Their hair is long and tied back with ribbons or bound in a net. Slaves and women in mourning have short hair.

MARRIED AT FOURTEEN? In ancient Greece, girls married as teenagers, often in arranged marriages. Before she married, a girl would give up her childhood toys to the twin Greek gods Artemis and Apollo. A Greek bride then took a ritual bath in water poured from a *loutrophoros* (a long-necked vase). The following evening, her husband and his "best man" collected her in a cart to go to her mother-in-law's house where they were showered with dates, nuts, figs, and cakes.

A Closer Look

• Notice the groom's "best man" facing backward in the cart.
• How many different things can you find women doing on Greek vases?

Black-figured Lekythos: Wedding Procession, Bridal Couple at Center, ca. 560 BC.

Sports and Games

Sports were an important part of the education of the wealthy classes in ancient Greece. Greek boys started to learn sports with a hired *paidotribe* (tutor) around the age of seven. After morning classes, the tutor took the boy to the gym, or *palaestra,* to practice wrestling, long jumping, running, and javelin and discus throwing. Scenes of young men working out with their trainers are common on all Greek vases. An essential part of an athlete's equipment was an *aryballos* (a tiny flask filled with olive oil used to protect skin from sun, dust, and scrapes) and a *strigil* (a metal scraper to clean off dust and dirt).

Myron, *Discobolus (Discus Thrower),* ca. 450 BC.

The skinny on sports Young athletes exercised in the nude in ancient Greece. What do you think were the benefits of exercising without wearing clothes?

Did you Know...

BARING THE TRUTH   The ancient Greek traveler Pausanias wrote about an athlete who changed the rules for ancient Greek sportswear. He tied his loincloth loosely so that it would fall off during a race, which allowed him to run faster. After he won the race, it was decided that clothes were unnecessary in athletic competitions.

Word Wizard

Gymnasium   *Gymnasium* derives from the ancient Greek word *gymnos* which meant "naked."

The Olympic Games—The Greek Sporting Legacy

The Olympic Games, held at Olympia, was the oldest Greek athletic competition. The event was held every four years to honor Zeus. The first Olympics, in 776 BC, consisted of a single footrace. Eventually, the event was expanded to include boxing, chariot races, the *pentathlon,* a race in armor, and a very rough wrestling contest called the *pankration.* All warfare stopped during the five-day summer event. Contestants had to swear to Zeus that they had trained hard for ten months. The Olympic Games stopped after the Romans conquered Greece in the second century AD, but were revived in 1896.

Prizes from Nature Winners in the ancient Olympic Games received a wreath of wild olive leaves. Victors in other Greek athletic games won crowns of pine needles and parsley! In the Panathenaic Games, the boy who won the wrestling championship received thirty jars of olive oil.

Did you Know...

Panathenaic vases were amphorae filled with olive oil. They were prizes in the Panathenaic Games, which were held once every four years at Athens in honor of Athena's birthday. The winner's sport is painted on one side. The other side shows Athena, patron goddess of Athens. Sometimes a Panathenaic vase bears a message that says, "I am one of the prizes from Athens." Panathenaic vases are always painted in black-figure style.

*Panathenaic prize amphora,
520–510 BC.*

A Closer Look

• What vase type is this?
• What sport did the athlete win?
• What color are the athletes painted? What is the natural clay color?
• Is there a Panathenaic vase in your museum gallery? For what sport was it a prize?
• Can you find a strigil or an aryballos in your museum's collection?

A pasta connection? Many Olympic champions came from the Greek colonies in Sicily in south Italy. Sicily was agriculturally richer than Greece. Some people suggest Italian Greek athletes were more successful than those from mainland Greece because they were better fed.

Ancient Coins

Many ancient Greek coins were buried for safekeeping and therefore have survived to be part of museum collections today. The Greeks may have first learned about coins from Lydia, an ancient country in west Asia, much of which is Turkey today. Each Greek city-state minted its own design. Coins were made of gold, silver, bronze, and electrum, an alloy of gold and silver.

An ancient Greek coin, called a *tetradrachm,* shows Athena on one side and her owl on the other. Notice Athena's olive branch and a crescent moon on this very early coin. Fifth century BC.

■ Look for turtles on coins from Aegina and for dolphins on coins from Argos.
■ Can you find the winged horse, Pegasus, from Corinth?

Boot Camp: Preparing for War

Greece was a single country united by one language, but it was made up of individual city-states that fought one another from time to time. Athletic training ensured that young men would be in good shape if they were called upon to fight. At age 18, young men entered military service for two years of training. Most of the Greek army was made up of shield-bearing foot soldiers. They were called *hoplites* after the shields (*hoplon*) that they carried.

Shields Thirty inches in diameter and weighing about twenty pounds, shields had a wood or hard leather core and were covered with bronze or leather. They had two grips for the left arm and hand.

Greaves These metal leg or shin guards were laced onto a soldier's leg.

Spears and daggers Hoplites carried a thrusting spear about eight to ten feet long and, sometimes, a shorter thrusting sword or dagger.

Helmets There were several different styles of helmet in ancient Greece. The Corinthian helmet, the most popular, had a nose guard and a crest of dyed horsehair.

■ Find armor on vase paintings: greaves, helmets, shields, and spears.

■ Look for signs of ancient battle in dents and cracks on helmets.

■ Look for tiny nail holes which secured a leather lining inside a helmet.

■ Find holes in greaves for laces to tie them to a soldier's leg.

Greek Art in Our Time

Sex symbols of ancient Greece The universal sign for female derives from Aphrodite's hand mirror. The sign for male came from Ares' shield and spear.

Male symbol   Female symbol

What's your sign? Is your birthday between July 23 and August 22? If so, your zodiac sign is Leo. Leo represents the Nemean lion strangled by Herakles in his first labor. To reward Herakles for his work, Zeus threw the lion's skin into the sky as a shiny trophy. Many zodiac signs and the names of constellations have their origins in Greek myths.

Flower power: Iris Sometimes seen on Greek vases, Iris was the goddess of the rainbow. As Hera's messenger, she traveled the rainbow to do her work. The colored part of our eyes is named after her as is the iris flower, which grows in many gardens.

Narcissus Our sweet-smelling spring flower got its name from the myth of Narcissus, who admired his reflection in a pond so much that he was punished for his vanity and turned into a flower. The narcissus flower grows well near water.

THE CLASSICAL

Roman art is often dismissed as a pale shadow of Greek art. The Romans were admirers of Greek art, but, while the Greeks aimed to show the ideal person in art, the Romans succeeded in revealing people as they were, warts and all. The Greeks looked to gods and heroes for their models. The Romans used their rulers and politicians as models in art. In architecture, where the Greeks lavished attention on building exteriors, the Romans explored new techniques of brickwork and concrete, and inlaid colored marble to create public buildings with grand interiors.

Greek Olympian Gods and their Roman Counterparts

Greek	Roman
Zeus (king of Gods)	Jupiter
Hera (Zeus' wife)	Juno
Demeter (Zeus' sister)	Ceres
Hades (Zeus' brother)	Pluto
Poseidon (Zeus' brother)	Neptune
Athena (Zeus' daughter)	Minerva
Hephaistus (Zeus and Hera's son)	Vulcan
Ares (Zeus and Hera's son)	Mars
Hermes (Zeus' son)	Mercury
Apollo (Zeus and Leto's son)	Apollo
Artemis (Apollo's twin)	Diana
Aphrodite (Zeus' daughter-in-law; Hephaistus' wife)	Venus

After the Romans conquered Greece in the second century BC, they adopted the twelve Greek Olympian gods. The gods kept their responsibilities, but all except Apollo were given new names.

CONNECTION

I can't tell Greek and Roman art apart! It's not easy! After the Romans conquered Greece in the second century AD, they brought home thousands of Greek sculptures for their public buildings and homes. Greek art became the rage in Rome. "Bring back some Greek sculptures," one Roman wrote. "The sooner the better; the more the merrier." Wealthy art patrons hired Greek and Roman artisans to copy classical Greek art for them. Also, Romans portrayed hair on their sculptures with deep holes made by boring drills.

How *can* you tell a Roman copy? Romans made many marble copies of Greek bronze sculptures. Marble copies needed struts (supporting bars) for added strength. Greek bronzes didn't require struts. Also, Romans portrayed hair on their sculptures with deep holes made by boring drills.

A telltale strut from a Roman copy of a Greek statuette. *Herakles* (detail), 5th century BC.

PURRR-FECT...ROMAN COPYCATS!

We have Romans to thank for keeping the legacy of Greek sculpture alive. If it weren't for Roman copyists, most museum visitors today would not know what ancient Greek sculpture looked like. Most Greek sculptures have disappeared, but Roman copies provide close likenesses of the originals.

ROMAN ART: AN OVERVIEW

While Greece was establishing colonies in south Italy in the seventh century BC, scattered settlements near the Tiber River in central Italy had banded together to form the ancient city of Rome. In less than five hundred years, Rome would conquer Greece and emerge as one of the great civilizations of the ancient world. Eventually, the Roman Empire, unified by temples, walls, public baths, and roads, would sprawl from the moors of Scotland to the Persian Gulf.

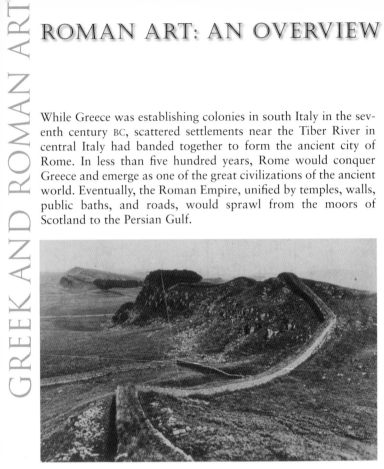

Hadrian's Wall in northern England was named after Roman Emperor Hadrian who ordered the wall built in 122 AD.

ART OOPS!

The Empire strikes back! Bombs dropped from warplanes in World War II blasted holes that uncovered important Roman ruins in London and Germany.

Thrown to the wolves Rome's name may come from the legend of Romulus and Remus. These twin sons of the war god, Mars, were abandoned by their mother at birth. A she-wolf found and raised them. As adults, they decided to build a city and agreed that the one who saw more vultures in flight could choose its location. Romulus saw more, and the city he built was named Rome after him.

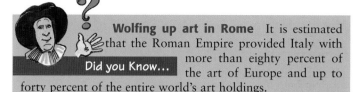
Pre-Roman, or Etruscan, Art

The seeds of Roman culture were sown in Etruria, a section of central Italy. Scholars debate whether the Etruscans came from Turkey or were native to Italy. A league of twelve cities by the seventh century BC, Etruria grew rich from its copper, silver, lead, tin, and iron deposits. Etruscan kings dominated Rome until the end of the sixth century BC.

Buried Treasure Most Etruscan art comes from tombs that were cut into hillsides and ridges outside their towns. Tomb chambers contained gifts for the dead to use in the next world. Many Etruscan tombs and their contents have remained intact because the rock-cut tombs are hard to get to and ruggedly built.

Etruscan tomb.

The Etruscan connection Etruscan priests forecast the future by studying the innards of sacrificial animals as well as patterns made by lightning and flying birds. The Romans later adopted some of these practices. Roman gladiator fights may have grown out of duels held at Etruscan funerals. Roman togas were inspired by the attire of Etruscan officials.

Did you Know...

A sarcophagus or coffin

Etruscan sarcophagus lids sometimes show a man and wife reclining together. Unlike the Greeks, Etruscans kept their clothes on in art and enjoyed parties with their wives.

Word Wizard

Sarcophogus (sar-kof-ah-gus) comes from the Greek *sarco* = flesh + *phaigen* = food. Meaning "flesh eater," a sarcophagus is a coffin.

GOLD JEWELRY

Gold bracelets, brooches, earrings, and necklaces made of tiny gold balls soldered to a support were an Etruscan specialty. This technique is called *granulation*.

METALWORK

Statuettes, animals, bronze mirrors, and safety pins (called *fibulae*), are common in museum collections.

CINERARY URNS

Ashes of the Etruscan dead were put into small terra-cotta boxes shaped like a house or temple. The lids of these small chests have an image of the person whose ashes are inside. Men are depicted holding libation bowls or writing materials. Women hold fans, mirrors, and sometimes pomegranates. The lids were often painted but the colors have worn off in damp underground chambers.

Etruscan, *Cinerary Urn*. An image of the deceased person on the lid of this urn shows him extending an offering bowl to the gods.

A Closer Look

• Note the purple stripe on the Etruscan figure's robe. Roman senators later had stripes like this on their clothing.

• Does your museum have an Etruscan sarcophagus?

• Locate metal statuettes, a cinerary urn, and gold jewelry.

• Look for figures wearing a cloak with a curved hem. The Romans later adopted this garment as their toga.

ROMAN SCULPTURE AND ARCHITECTURE

Roman Portrait Sculpture

The Romans made a unique contribution to art through portrait sculpture. It is thought that the ancient Roman custom of keeping wax death masks of family members gave them an appreciation for "true" likenesses. The perishable nature of wax masks eventually led to a demand for equally true-to-life sculptures of stone.

Bust of a Roman, 1st century BC.

Where did the Romans get marble for sculpture? They used some Greek marble and the pure white marble from Cararra in northern Italy. They also imported dozens of varieties of colored marble from western Asia and Africa.

Masks

Death masks   The Romans made wax masks of family members shortly after their deaths. Death masks were painted to look like the deceased, stored at home and taken out at funerals, state occasions, and sacrifices. Called *imagines,* they were sometimes worn by actors playing the part of an ancestor. Death masks allowed ancestors to be "present" at family occasions. They also served to remind young family members of their bloodlines. The custom of making death masks dates from at least the second century BC.

Life masks   In later times, the Romans made masks of important living people while they were still alive. Wax or plaster would be applied to the person's face after breathing tubes or straws were put into the nostrils to make breathing possible. After the wax or plaster hardened, the mask was removed and could be used as a mold for a terra-cotta or bronze bust of the person.

True portraits The Romans did not hide plain features and ugly flaws in their busts and statues. Moles, wrinkles, pouches, folded skin, and bald heads were common in early Roman portrait sculpture. Civic-minded Romans admired a face that expressed the wisdom of old age, an air of responsibility, and a no-nonsense approach to life.

TOGA TALK Worn by free-born Roman male citizens, togas were eighteen feet long and four and a half feet wide. They were worn draped over a tunic. Boys were allowed to wear the white toga of adulthood around the age of eighteen. Senators' togas had a purple stripe on the edge.

Roman with Two Masks. This sculpture shows the Roman custom of taking ancestors' death masks to funerals.

A Closer Look

• Does the Roman above look like someone you know? Maybe a neighbor or a teacher?

• Compare a Roman portrait to a Greek portrait. How are they different? To whom would you rather speak?

• How do we remember our ancestors today?

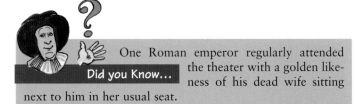

Did you Know... One Roman emperor regularly attended the theater with a golden likeness of his dead wife sitting next to him in her usual seat.

Portraits of the Emperor

The emperor at work Many museums have portrait sculptures of Roman emperors. Roman imperial workshops made thousands of emperor statues that were shipped out to distant parts of the empire so people there would know what their ruler looked like. The emperor's image decorated temples, theaters, baths, gardens, libraries, and gymnasia from England to Egypt. Portraits of the emperor's wife and family were also sent around the empire. Art was used as propaganda, or advertising to promote the emperor's political power to the general public.

Augustus of Prima Porta, ca. 20 BC. In his time, Augustus (ruled 27 BC–14 AD) was the most sculpted man in the Western world. Emperor for forty-one years, he is shown here addressing his army. Venus' son, Cupid, rides a dolphin at Augustus' feet. He is a reminder that Augustus was believed to be descended from Venus.

A **Closer Look**

- Look for the parts of Augustus' armor—breastplate and leather fringe.
- Find an emperor's portrait in sculpture.
- If your museum has marble portraits of Roman emperors, compare them. Which would you want as your ruler?

The emperor's clothes

The emperor wearing the armor of the Roman army was a favorite subject for sculptors. Roman soldiers wore leather-lined breastplates over short woolen tunics. The leather lining ended in long fringe strips. Two rows of metal plates hung from each breastplate. The sound of the metal plates clanking when the army was on the march was designed to be frightening. Soldiers wore boots or sandals.

Did you Know... A Roman soldier carried between sixty and ninety pounds of equipment when he marched. Not only did he carry his armor, shield, and lance but also a woolen cloak, bottle of water, sickle, chain, bucket, ax, saw, and basket. Roman soldiers did more than fight. They were expected to dig roads, build walls, and fortify camps.

The emperor's monster in Roman art

Combining a lion's strength with an eagle's vigilance, the griffin was a symbol of the emperor's power.

OFF WITH HIS HEAD!

It wasn't practical to carve many thousands of new emperor sculptures each time a new emperor took office. It was easier to slip new heads into an already carved suit of armor. Replacement heads have a curved line at the base of the neck.

EYE WITNESS

You can guess when an emperor ruled by looking at the eyes in his portrait sculpture. If his pupil and iris are incised (scratched) into the stone, he probably ruled after Hadrian, whose reign ended in 138 AD. If the eyeball has no markings, the emperor probably ruled before that time.

Art "bust"

Greek sculptors carved full-body sculptures, but the Romans preferred busts. A bust is a sculpture of a person's head and shoulders. The term *bust* comes from Italian, *busto,* meaning "upper body."

Whiskers and beards in Roman art The emperor was the pacesetter for upper-class fashion. Courtiers even copied their emperor's facial hair! Augustus was clean-shaven, as were his courtiers. But when Hadrian grew a short beard, upper-class men grew beards, too. Art reflects these trends. Portrait sculptures during Augustus' rule show clean-shaven men; when Hadrian ruled, portraits had clipped beards. Beards stayed in style until Constantine the Great, when a clean shave, in life and art was back in style.

Bust of Septimius Severus, ca. 201-210 AD.

A   Closer Look

• Do you prefer your emperor to be bearded or shaved?

• In your museum, try to guess by beard or eyes roughly when an emperor might have lived.

Emperors up close and personal Domitian (ruled 81–96 AD) could not bear the sound of splashing oars. On water, he was towed in a separate boat out of earshot of the oarsmen. **Augustus** rarely bathed in winter; he was oiled, sweated before a fire, and rinsed with water. **Diocletian** (ruled 284–305 AD) grew cabbages after he retired. **Tiberius** (ruled 14–37 AD) kept pet snakes. **Hadrian** was a painter and sculptor. He went regularly to the public baths where he once gave three slaves to a penniless man sitting next to him. **Marcus Aurelius** (ruled 161–180 AD) took painting lessons. **Caligula** (ruled 37–41 AD) means "Baby Boots." He got the name as a baby after his father, a Roman consul, paraded him in a tiny soldier's outfit—boots and all—in front of the Roman army.

What language did the emperors speak? Latin was the official language of the Roman empire.

Women's Portraits in Roman Art

Women were draped in Roman art. They wore a *stola* (a loose tunic similar to a Greek chiton) and a *palla* (a rectangular wool shawl similar to a Greek himation) resting around their shoulders or pulled over their heads.

Hair-raising art In Roman art, you can guess when a woman lived by her hair. Wealthy Roman women often

Did you Know...

copied the hairstyle of the ruling emperor's wife. For instance, the towering hairdo of Emperor Domitian's wife, Domitia, was imitated in court circles. A sculpture of a woman with soaring tiers of curls suggests that the Roman lady lived around the time of Domitia.

Portrait of a Lady, ca. 90 AD. Notice the piled-high hair carved on this bust of a woman. The eyes and lips on this sculpture would have been painted.

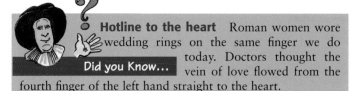

Hotline to the heart Roman women wore wedding rings on the same finger we do today. Doctors thought the vein of love flowed from the fourth finger of the left hand straight to the heart.

Did you Know...

How did Roman women create their hairstyles?
Trained slaves or hairdressers arranged women's hair with curling irons.

A Closer Look

• Can you find three different Roman women's hairstyles in your museum?
• Find a palla or a stola.

Children's Portraits in Roman Art

The Romans were gifted at sculpting children. They captured their innocence and the soft skin and chubby contours of their faces. Public statues were made of the emperor's children and grandchildren. Many children died in those days. Museum collections have portraits of children from family tombs. In some of the portraits, the children are holding a favorite pet.

Small Boy of the Intro-Claudian period, ca. 50 AD.

■ Look for children in Roman art.
■ Guess their age and then check their date of birth and death.

Roman Gods

As you know, the Romans adopted the twelve Greek Olympian gods and gave them new names. The Romans also had their own gods. *Lares* were spirits who looked after the Roman household. *Penates* were gods who guarded the food supply. Images of these gods were kept in a household shrine where they were given daily offerings.

In time, Romans tired of the Olympian gods they adopted from Greece and tried new ones. Mithras, an ancient Persian god of light, and Isis, an Egyptian goddess of magic, became popular. Christians were not allowed to worship until the fourth century AD, when the emperor Constantine the Great made Christianity the official religion of the Roman Empire.

This *lare* is shown pouring wine and holding a libation or offering to the gods.

Constantine the Great was the first emperor in two hundred years not to wear a beard. His head is eight feet high in this sculpture, ca. 330 AD.

A Closer Look

• In your museum, find an image of a major Roman god and, then, one of his or her Greek counterpart. (Turn to page 16 for help.)
• Do the two wear or carry the same emblem?
• In your museum, look for bronze lares that are about seven inches high.

Think Big!

The Romans were great builders. They built Greek-style temples dedicated to emperors and gods, but turned to concrete and brickwork to construct public buildings on a grand scale. These materials enabled them to design vast interior spaces using arches, vaults, and domes. Basilicas and baths, central to Roman social life, owed their final forms to concrete, as did amphitheaters such as the Colosseum. The Romans also excelled at public works. Aqueducts and bridges were part of the fabric of the empire. Closer to home, the first "high-rises" were built to house Rome's many people.

Giovanni Paolo Panini, *Interior of the Pantheon, Rome,* ca. 1734. The Pantheon (ca. 126 AD) was designed with the help of Emperor Hadrian. This circular temple with a concrete dome honored all the gods of the Roman Empire, and is the finest of all existing Roman temples.

A temple toss-up? If the Parthenon is considered the symbol of Athens, the Pantheon is the symbol of Rome.

A concrete invention! The Romans made concrete from sand and stones mixed with limestone mortar, which was mostly volcanic dust and water. It was cheap and strong. Just think—concrete mixers rumbling around today are stirring a 2000-year-old recipe.

Did you Know...

CAPITAL IDEAS The Romans used all three orders of Greek columns, but added two more called *Composite* and *Tuscan*. A Composite column combines Ionic scrolls and Corinthian acanthus leaves. A Tuscan column is a squat version of a Doric column. The Corinthian was the most popular column used for large buildings.

Roman emperor's victory arch.

A common Roman decorative motif used in architecture and relief sculpture was the *rinceau*, or vine, motif. It looks like leafy foliage. (Turn to page 52 to see an example.)

Did you Know...

■ Does your museum have any Roman columns?
■ Look for the vine motif in Roman sculpture.

Pompeii

When Mt. Vesuvius erupted near the Roman seaside town of Pompeii, it was one o'clock in the afternoon, August 24, 79 AD. Modestus, a baker, had just put eighteen loaves of bread in the oven. Some priests were sitting down to a lunch of almonds, hazelnuts, eggs, dates, and bread. Families were eating in restaurants. Suddenly, the sky turned black, and within hours Pompeii was buried under more than eighteen feet of volcanic ash.

J.M.W. Turner, *Vesuvius in Eruption*, 1817.

A petrifying place   Pompeii was discovered in the late sixteenth century, and excavations began in 1748. Excavations reveal what people were doing when the lava covered them. Bodies, long decomposed, have left holes in the hard volcanic ash that surrounded them. Archaeologists have filled some holes with plaster to make casts of peoples' final moments before they were covered with lava. They have recreated children crouching in fear, dogs running, and a woman with three servants fleeing with jewels and silver.

This dog was a victim of Mt. Vesuvius' eruption in Pompeii.

BRIGHTEN YOUR SMILE WITH VOLCANIC ASH!

Chances are that your dentist uses volcanic ash, known as pumice, to clean your teeth. Certainly, your parents' teeth were cleaned with pumice. Today, some dentists use synthetic pumice instead.

Word Wizard

Vulcanologist   An expert on volcanos. The name comes from Vulcan, the Roman god of fire.

Wall paintings

Most surviving Roman wall paintings were found in private Roman houses in towns such as Pompeii that were buried by the eruption of Mt. Vesuvius. Preserved by volcanic lava, some are almost as fresh as when they were painted almost two thousand years ago. Windows were rare in Roman houses, so painted murals were used to brighten and decorate the interiors. Architectural scenes created a feeling of greater space, while landscapes brought the outside world indoors. Some murals were still lifes of food and tableware.

How were wall paintings made? Plaster was combined with marble dust and laid down in layers over a smoothed wall. Paint was applied to either wet or dry plaster. This technique is called *fresco*.

Villa Boscoreale, 1st century BC.

A Closer Look

• Find two features of Roman architecture in the above painting. (arch and Corinthian-style column)
• What has the artist done to take our eyes back into space?

Some grated cheese with your art? Some frescos have been shipped to museums packed in grated Parmesan cheese. The moisture and padding of the cheese helps preserve the plaster and paint.

LIFE IN ANCIENT ROME

Mosaics

The Romans were skilled at making pictures from small colored pieces of pottery, glass, tile, or stone set in plaster or concrete. These designs were called mosaics, or "work of the muses." The Romans didn't use rugs. Instead, mosaics decorated floors, walls, and ceilings in private houses and public baths. Like the Greeks, Romans reclined on their sides during meals and ate with their hands. Garbage, such as shells and bones, was thrown on the floor.

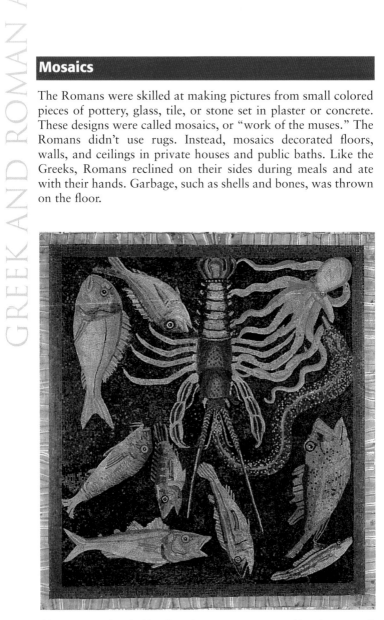

This ancient mosaic shows food from the Mediterranean Sea—octopus, spiny lobster, bass, moray eel, and scorpionfish.

SOMETHING FISHY

Romans liked serving their foods with sauces. Sauces made dull foods interesting and disguised "spoiled" foods. One popular sauce was called *garum,* which was made by fermenting fish innards and salty water. Garum was stored in amphorae and traded to other countries. Archaeologists have found storage depots for garum in Pompeii.

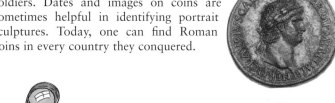

Dying for supper The oldest complete cookbook in history was written by a Roman, Marcus Gavius Apicius, in the first century AD. It was called *The Art of Cookery.* Some recipes were:

Did you Know...

- Roast parrot
- Jellyfish and eggs
- Dormice stuffed with pork and pine kernels

Coins in Roman Art

Gold, silver, and bronze coins were minted to show people in the Roman Empire what their emperor looked like. The reverse of the coin was used to advertise the emperor's achievements. Triumphal arches, bridges, and roads were common themes. Coins were also made to pay soldiers. Dates and images on coins are sometimes helpful in identifying portrait sculptures. Today, one can find Roman coins in every country they conquered.

A   Closer Look

- What was on the back of Nero's coin? Why?
- Find a coin showing a well-known Roman emperor, such as Augustus. Can you match it with a portrait sculpture of the same emperor?

Sestertius of Nero, 64–66 AD. This Roman coin shows the head of Nero wearing a laurel wreath on one side. A triumphal arch is on the other side.

Roman Legacy

Months of the year January is named for the two-faced god of doors, gates, and beginnings, **Janus.** March is named for the war god, **Mars,** because March was when the Romans started their military campaigns. July is named for **Julius Caesar,** and August is named for Caesar's adopted son, Octavian, who later became the emperor **Augustus.**

Phrase fiend: Janus-faced
Hypocrites are described as two-faced or Janus-faced because they "face" two ways at once.

Coin, ca. 350 BC.

Planets

The planets in our solar system are named for some of the Roman gods and goddesses. Make a line to connect the description of each planet with its god.

Venus	fastest moving and closest to the sun
Jupiter	farthest away in black night sky
Pluto	greenish-blue like the sea
Mercury	brightest and most beautiful
Neptune	largest planet

ROMAN NUMERALS The Romans gave us the seven Roman numerals: I(1), V(5), X(10), L(50), C(100), D(500), and M(1000). Where do we use them? On monuments, on some clocks, in some book chapter headings, on some encyclopedia volumes, and to number the Super Bowl games!

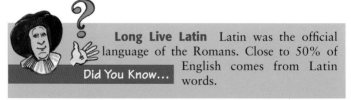

Long Live Latin Latin was the official language of the Romans. Close to 50% of English comes from Latin words.

Did You Know...

ACTIVITIES

Mnemonics

Mnemonics (pronounced ni-*mon*-icks) are word tricks used to help us remember certain things. Words and letters can jog your memory. You can use mnemonics to remember highlights of a museum visit.

MUD   Use the letters in the word MUD to think of three things: Materials (what something is made of), Use (what it was used for), and Design (how it is decorated). As you look at something you like in Greek or Roman art, play with MUD.

M   Materials   What material is it made of? Is it stone, clay, or bronze?

U   Use   What do you think the object was used for? For the tomb? For the house? For worship? For propaganda?

D   Design or decoration   Is the object brightly painted or plain? Is the design carved into or added onto the surface? If you took away the design or decoration, how would it change the look and feel of the object?

M&M   Think M&M when you are looking at Greek art. Bring an M&Ms wrapper to the museum with you. Hold it up. Let it remind you of the two major themes in Greek art: man and myths.

Hunts

Any of the following will give you a way to focus and a chance to look around your museum—and they're fun!

"Mug shot" or face hunt
- Find an archaic smile and almond eyes on a Greek sculpture.
- Find a Roman nose. Does it look like an eagle's beak?
- Check for wrinkles, lines, and pouches on Roman faces. Do the people look real?

- Find old people's faces in Roman art. Can you find old faces in Greek art?
- Look for incised eyes in Roman art. Look for blank eyes in Greek art. (Reminder: Greeks painted their statues' eyes, but did not generally incise them.)

Column hunt
- Look for columns in your museum.
- Look for columns painted on Greek vases.
- Turn a coin over. See any columns? What kind? Try a penny, nickel, and (if you're lucky) a twenty-dollar bill.
- Look on the front of a one-dollar bill and a five-dollar bill. Spot the Roman vine motif along the borders.

Hair and beard hunt
- Find beards in Roman art.
- Find drill holes in Roman hairdos.
- Compare a Greek god's hair with a Roman emperor's hair.

God hunt
- Find a depiction of a Greek god. Can you locate the matching Roman god? Do they look alike?
- How many Greek gods can you find? Write down their names.

Monster hunt
- Find a griffin.
- Find a sphinx.
- Find a centaur.
- Find a gorgon head. (Hint: Look on Athena's breastplate or shield.)
- Find the Minotaur.

Hand-of-the-artist hunt
- Look for signatures on Greek vases. Look for the words *epoison* and *egraphsen*.
- Look for a love inscription or *kalos*.

Coin hunt
- Match an emperor's head on a Roman coin with a sculpture of the same emperor.
- Find a bearded emperor and a clean-shaven emperor on a coin.
- Find a coin with a Greek or Roman god or goddess on it.
- How many animals can you find on Greek coins?

Making Art

In the style of... Give yourself a name such as the "big eye" painter. Draw a Greek vase scene in the style that gave you your name.

The shape of the vase Draw the outline of a Greek vase you like. Label the lip, shoulder, neck, belly, and foot. Then, design a new shape for a vase. What would it be used for?

Name that motif Invent a decorative motif for a Greek vase (such as the meander), and name it.

Everyday scene Find a Greek pot you like and draw its outline. Fill it with a scene from your everyday life.

Trace it Make a silhouette.

For luck Draw a round shield and decorate it with a good luck symbol.

Change for a dollar? Design a coin.

Writing

- Create and describe a new Greek or Roman god or goddess. What area of life do they rule? What items do they carry?
- Describe a new Greek monster with at least two animal parts.
- Look up the sign of the zodiac under which you were born. Write a myth about how your sign got into the sky.
- Write a VASE poem. Use the letters **V, A, S,** and **E** to begin four lines of poetry. Here's a example:

    Very old
    Art with few colors
    Someone's treasure long ago
    Everyone now admires.

- Ask at your museum's information desk how to find a European painting of a classical myth. Look at the painting and write down the title and artist. Write what you think happens in the myth portrayed in the painting. Then, find and read the classical myth. How does your myth compare with the classical version?

Antique Fish

This is one of the first published recipes in history. It was created by a famous Greek chef. Choose any fish *you* like. You might want to add a favorite ingredient to bring the recipe into the twentieth century.

1. Cut off the head of a ribbon fish.
2. Wash it and cut into slices.
3. Pour cheese and oil over it.

Athena's Dip

All of the following ingredients, except the cream cheese, were available in ancient Greece.

      8 ounces cream cheese
      small bottle of stuffed olives
      2 hard-boiled eggs
      1–2 tablespoons chopped onion

Mix the ingredients together and serve on crackers.

CREDITS

PAGE

cover Greek, Attic, *Nolan Amphora,* ca. 450–440 BC. Ceramic, red-figure, h: 13" x d: 6½" (33.2 x 16.7 cm). Bequest of Mrs. Martin Brimmer, Courtesy Museum of Fine Arts, Boston. Photograph ©2000 Museum of Fine Arts, Boston. All rights reserved.

2 Rembrandt van Rijn, *Artist in His Studio,* ca. 1629. Oil on panel, 9¾ x 12½" (24.8 x 31.7 cm). Zoe Oliver Sherman Collection. Given in memory of Lillie Oliver Poor. Courtesy Museum of Fine Arts, Boston.

8 *Peplos Kore,* ca. 6th c. BC. Marble. Courtesy the Museum of Classical Archaeology, Cambridge, England.

9 *Oinochoe (Geometric pitcher),* 8th c. BC. Ceramic, h: 13" (33.1 cm). Perkins Collection, Courtesy Museum of Fine Arts, Boston. Photograph ©1999 Museum of Fine Arts, Boston. All rights reserved.

11 Exekias, *Amphora,* Black-figure vase. Purchased by Contribution. Courtesy, Museum of Fine Arts, Boston. ©1999 Museum of Fine Arts, Boston. All rights reserved.

11 *Charioteer of Delphi,* ca. 475–470 BC. Bronze, height: 71" (180 cm). Courtesy Davis Art Slides.

12 Engraving of Aeneas escaping from Troy. From *Die Westgeschichte fur Kinder (Children's History of the World).* Nurmberg, 1928.

13 *Sophie Schliemann,* ca. 1892. Photo courtesy Bildarchiv Preussischer Kultur-besitz, Berlin. Reproduced with permission.

15 George F. Watts, *The Minotaur,* 1885. Tate Gallery, London, Great Britain. Tate Gallery, London/Art Resource, NY.

16 Late Hellinistic or Greco-Roman, *Head of Homer.* Marble, h: 16" (41 cm). Henry Lillie Pierce Fund. Courtesy the Museum of Fine Arts, Boston. Photograph ©1999 Museum of Fine Arts, Boston. All rights reserved.

18 Antimenes Painter, *Neck Amphora (View of Hermes with Hera, Athena, and Aphrodite),* ca. 525 BC. Ceramic, black-figure vase, h: 17½" (44 cm). Seth K. Sweetser Fund. Courtesy Museum of Fine Arts, Boston. Photograph ©1999 Museum of Fine Arts, Boston. All rights reserved.

19 *Black-figured Amphora,* side A: Birth of Athena, ca. 540 BC. Terra cotta, h: 16¾" x d: 11¼" (42.5 x 28.5 cm). Virginia Museum of Fine Arts, Richmond. The Arthur and Margaret Glasgow Fund. Photo: Katherine Wetzel. © Virginia Museum of Fine Arts.

20 Christophe Schwarz, *The Abduction of Persephone,* ca. 1570. Oil on canvas, 26 x 37¾" (66 x 95.9 cm). Photograph © The Fitzwilliam Museum, University of Cambridge. no. 1778.

21 Jon Roddam Spencer-Stanhope, *Psyche and Charon.* Courtesy Roy Miles Esq./Bridgeman Art Library, London.

22 Ancient Greek, Attic (attributed to Paseas), Plate: *Herakles, Hermes, and Cerberus,* ca. 520 BC. Red-figure vase, d: 7½" (19 cm). Henry Lillie Pierce Fund, Courtesy, Museum of Fine Arts, Boston. ©1999, Museum of Fine Arts, Boston. All rights reserved.

25 *Herakles and Boar.* Black-figure vase. Courtesy the British Museum, London.

26 Greek, Attic, *Nolan Amphora,* ca. 450–440 BC. Ceramic, red-figure, h: 13" x d: 6½" (33.2 x 16.7 cm). Bequest of Mrs. Martin Brimmer, Courtesy Museum of Fine Arts, Boston. Photograph ©2000 Museum of Fine Arts, Boston. All rights reserved.

27 *Women Bearing Grave Offering,* ca. 450–420 BC. Ceramic (white ground lekythos), 15 x 4⅝" (38.1 x 11.7 cm). Catharine Page Perkins Fund, Courtesy, Museum of Fine Arts, Boston. Photograph ©1999 Museum of Fine Arts, Boston. All rights reserved.

28 Ancient Greece, *Kylix Attic Black-figure Eye Cup,* ca. 520–500 BC. Terracotta, h: 4"; d: 8½" (h: 10; d: 22 cm). Museum Purchase, AP1966.28.1. The Cummer Museum of Art & Gardens, Jacksonville, FL.

32 Greece, Late Archaic, *Head of a Man* (detail), 480 BC. Marble. Charles Amos Cummings Fund, Courtesy Museum of Fine Arts, Boston. ©1999 Museum of Fine Arts, Boston. All rights reserved.

32 Polykleitos, *Doryphoros,* ca. 450–440 BC. Marble (copy after bronze original), H: 5'8" (178 cm). Courtesy Davis Art Slides.

33 Greek (Hellenistic), *Wrestlers,* late 2nd c. BC. Bronze. Courtesy The Walters Art Gallery, Baltimore.

34 Iktinos and Kallikrates, *Parthenon,* 448–432 BC. The Acropolis, Athens, Greece. Courtesy the Greek Tourist Authority.

36 Foundry Painter (attributed to), *Kylix* (detail: interior—man and youth on couch), about 480 BC. Ceramic, red-figure, H: 4½" x D: 11¼" (11.7 x 29.8 cm). Henry Lillie Pierce Fund. Courtesy, Museum of Fine Arts, Boston. © 1999. Museum of Fine Arts, Boston. All rights reserved.

38 *Amphora* (View: side B: Dionysus drinking wine), ca. 540 BC. Ceramic, black-figure vase, h: 20½" (52 cm). H.L. Pierce Fund and Francis Bartlett Collection. Courtesy The Museum of Fine Arts, Boston. Photograph ©1999 Museum of Fine Arts, Boston. All rights reserved.

39 Attributed to the Amasis Painter, *Black-figured Lekythos: Wedding Procession, Bridal couple at center,* ca. 560 BC. The Metropolitan Museum of Art, Purchase, 1956, Walter C. Baker Gift. (56.11.1)

39 Myron, *Discobolos (Discus Thrower),* ca. 450 BC. (Roman copy of Greek original). Marble, life-sized. Museo Nazionale Romano delle Terme, Rome, Italy. Courtesy Scala/Art Resource, NY.

41 Greek, Attic, Attributed to the Leagros Group, *Panathenaic prize amphora* (side B: Horse Race), 520–510 BC. Black-figured vase, H: 25½" (64.8 cm). The Metropolitan Museum of Art, Rogers Fund, 1907. (07.286.80)

42 Ancient Greece, *Coin (tetradrachm) from Athens, Greece* (reverse: owl; obverse: head of Athena), 5th c. BC. Silver, diam: ½" (23.5 mm). Museum of Art and Archaeology, University of Missouri, Columbia, MO.

45 Graeco-Roman, *Herakles* (detail), 5th c. BC. Fine-grained marble with crystals, h: 57 m. Francis Bartlett Donation of 1912, Courtesy, Museum of Fine Arts, Boston. © 1999 Museum of Fine Arts, Boston. All rights reserved.

48 Etruscan, *Cinerary Urn.* Terracotta. Courtesy the British Museum, London.

49 Roman, *Bust of a Roman,* 1st c. BC. Marble, h: 14⅜" (36.5 cm). The Metropolitan Museum of Art, Rogers Fund, 1912. (12.233)

50 *Roman with Two Masks.* Marble. Courtesy the Capitoline Museum, Rome, Italy.

51 *Augustus of Prima Porta,* ca. 20 BC. Marble, h: 6'8" (2 m). Courtesy the Vatican Museum, Vatican City, Italy.

53 *Bust of Septimius Severus,* c. 201–210 AD. Marble, H: 25" (77 cm). Indiana University Art Museum: Gift of Thomas T. Solley. Photograph by Michael Cavanagh and Kevin Montague. © 2000 Indiana University Art Museum.

54 *Portrait of a Lady,* ca. 90 AD. Marble, life-size. Courtesy Capitoline Museum, Rome, Italy.

55 Roman Imperial, *Small Boy of the Intro-Claudian Period,* ca. 50 AD. Marble, h: 9½" (24.5 cm). Henry Lillie Pierce Fund. Courtesy the Museum of Fine Arts, Boston. Photograph © 1999 Museum of Fine Arts, Boston. All rights reserved.

56 *Lare.* Courtesy the British Museum, London.

56 *Constantine the Great,* about 330 AD. Marble, head about 8' ¼" (2.5 m) high. Palace of the Conservatory, Rome. Photo courtesy Ruthie Knapp.

57 Giovanni Paolo Panini, *Interior of the Pantheon, Rome,* ca. 1734. Oil on canvas, 50½ x 39" (128.3 x 99.1 cm).Samuel H. Kress Collection. Photo by Richard Carafelli. © 2000 Board of Trustees, National Gallery of Art, Washington, DC.

59 J. M. W. Turner, *Vesuvius in Eruption,* 1817. Watercolor and scraping out with some pen and ink on wove paper, 11¼ x 15½" (28.6 x 39.8 cm). Yale Center for British Art, Paul Mellon Collection. B1975.4.1857.

60 *Dog and human victim from the eruption of Mt. Vesuvius.* Photo courtesy the Imperial Tobacco Co.

61 Roman, Pompeian, *Villa Boscoreale* (detail: west wall panel), 1st c. BC. Fresco on lime plaster, h: 8' average (2.4 m). The Metropolitan Museum of Art, Rogers Fund, 1093. (03.14.13) Photograph © 1986 The Metropolitan Museum of Art.

62 Ancient Rome, *Assorted edible fish.* Mosaic. Courtesy the British Museum, London.

63 Roman Imperial, *Sestertius of Nero,* 64–66 AD. Bronze, diam: 1" (36 mm). Anonymous Gift in Memory of Zoe Wilbour. Courtesy, Museum of Fine Arts, Boston. © 1999 Museum of Fine Arts, Boston. All rights reserved.

64 Roman, *Coin* (obverse: Janus Head), ca. 350 BC. Bronze. Courtesy the Museum of Fine Arts, Boston. Photograph © 1999 the Museum of Fine Arts, Boston. All rights reserved.

INDEX

The Abduction of Persephone (Schwarz), **20**
acanthus, 29
accession numbers, 7
AD (Anno Domini), 6
alphabet, Greek, 20
Amphora, **38**
amphora, 25
Amphora (Exekias), **11**
Antimenes Painter, *The Judgment of Paris,* **18**
Aphrodite, 16
Apicius, Marcus Gavius, first cookbook, 63
Apollo, 16, 39
archaic sculpture, 31–32
archaeology, 12
  archaeological dig, 13
  property of objects, 14
architecture
  Greek, 34–35
  Roman, 57–61
Ares, 17
Artemis, 17, 39
artifact, 14
  maintenance, 6
Artist in His Studio (Rembrandt van Rijn), **2**
Athena, 17
  birth of, 19
  Birth of Athena, **19**
Augustus, 53
Augustus of Prima Porta, **51**

Bacchus, 37
BC (before Christ), 6
beards
  hunt, 66
  in Roman art, 53
bioturbation, 14
Birth of Athena, **19**
black-figure vase, 25
bust, 52
  Bust of Roman, **49**
  Bust of Septimius Severus, **53**

Caligula, 54
capital, 9

celebration, in ancient Greece, 36–38
centaur, 30
Ceres, 17
Charioteer of Delphi, **11**
Charon, 21
cinerary urn, 48, **48**
Clark, Sir Kenneth, 5
clay pottery, 14
coins
  Greek, 42
  hunt, 66
  Roman, 63, **64**
  Sestertius of Nero, **63**
  tetradrachm, **42**
color, 8
  Greek vases, 25–27
column, 9
  Greek, 35
  Roman, 58
composition, 10
Constantine the Great, **56**
contrapposto, 32–33
Corinthian order, 35
cottabos, 36
Cupid, 16

dagger, 43
dates, 6
death masks, 49
Demeter, 17
dentil, 29
design, 29
Diana, 17
Diocletian, 53
Dionysus, 37, 38
Discobolus (Discus Thrower) (Myron), **39**
Domitian, 53
Doric order, 35
Doryphoros (Polykleitos), **32**

emperor, portraits of, 51–54
Etruria, 47
  Etruscan tomb, **47**
Exekias, *Amphora,* **11**

fashion, in ancient Greece, 38
fresco, 60–61
frieze, 9

galleries, museum, 6
geometric style, 9
gods and goddesses, 15
  Greek and Roman counterparts, 44
  hunt, 66
  Roman, 56
gorgons, 30
greave, 42
Greek art, in museum, 15
griffin, 52
gymnasium, 40

Hades, 21
  Persephone's abduction by, 20
Hadrian, 52, 53, 54
  Hadrian's Wall, **46**
hairstyle
  comparison, 66
  Roman women, 54–55
Head of a Man, **32**
helmet, 43
HEPA (high-efficiency particle-arresting) filter, 6
Hera, 17
Herakles, 22
  Plate: Herakles, Hermes, & Cerberus, **22**
Herakles and Boar, black-figure vase, **25**
Hermes, 18
heroes and legends, 22
Hesiod, 20
Homer, 16
  Head of Homer, **16**
  Iliad, 12, 16
horizontal, 10
hunts, activities in museum, 65–66
hydria, 24
hygrometer, 6
hygrothermograph, 6

Iliad (Homer), 12, 16
  Trojan War in, 22
Ionic column/order, 9, 35
Iris, 43

jewelry, 48
The Judgment of Paris (Antimenes Painter), **18**
Juno, 17
Jupiter, 18

kantharos, 37
kore, 31
kouros, 31
krater, 37
Kylix, **36**
Kylix Atic Black-figure Eye cup, **28**

labels, 7
lare, 56, **56**
lekythos, 27, 39
life masks, 49
line, 10
lotus, 29
loutrophoros, 39

maintenance, artifacts, 6
Marcus Aurelius, 54
Mars, 17
masks, 49
meander, 10, 29
Mercury, 18
military life, ancient Greece, 42
Minerva, 17
The Minotaur (Watts), *15*
mnemonics, activities, 65
monster, 30
  hunt, 66
month, names, 64
mosaics, 62
museum, 4–5
Myron, *Discobolus (Discus Thrower),* **39**
myth, 20

Narcissus, 43
nudity, Greek sculpture, 15

Oinochoe, **9**, 37
Olympic Games, 40–41
Olympus, Mount, 16, 17
Ovid, 20

palmette leaves, 29
Panathenaic prize amphora, **41**
Panini, Giovanni Paolo, *Interior of the Pantheon, Rome,* 57

Pantheon, 58
  Interior of the Pantheon, Rome (Panini), **57**
Paris, *The Judgment of Paris,* 18
Parthenon, 9, 34
pattern, 29
pediment, 9
Peplos Kore, **8**
Persephone, 18
  abduction by Hades, 20
planets, names, 64
Pluto, 21
Polykleitos, *Doryphoros,* **32**
Pompeii, 59–61
Portrait of a Lady, **54**
portrait sculpture, 49–50
  children, 55
  emperors, 51–54
  women, 54
Proserpine, 18
Psyche and Charon (Spencer-Stanhoe), 21

recipes, 67
red-figure vase, 26
Rembrandt van Rijn, *Artist in His Studio,* **2**
rinceau, 59
Roman emperor's victory arch, **58**
Roman with Two Masks, **50**
Rome, naming of, 46

sarcophagus, 48
Schliemann, Heinrich, 12–13
Schliemann, Sophia, 13
Schwarz, Christophe, *The Abduction of Persephone,* **20**
sculpture, 11
  classical Greek, 32
  early Greek, 31
  hellenistic Greek, 33
  human body Greek, 15
  Roman portrait, 49–53
sex symbols, ancient Greek, 43
shape, 9
  Greek pots, 24
shield, 42
signature, 28
silhouette, 25

silica gel, 6
sirens, 30
Small Boy of the Intro-Claudian period, **55**
spear, 43
Spencer-Stanhoe, Jon Roddam, *Psyche and Charon,* 21
sphinx, 30
sports and games, 39–40
strut, 45
symposia, 36

temples, Greek, 34–35
terra cotta, 24
Tiberius, 53
toga, 50
Troy, 12–13
  Trojan War, 22
Turner, J. M. W., *Vesuvius in Eruption,* 59

vase
  black-figure, 25
  forms and categories of Greek, 23–24
  painting, 9
  red-figure, 26
  repair, 27
  white-ground, 27
Venus, 16
Vesuvius in Eruption (Turner), **59**
Villa Boscoreale, **61**
volute, 9

Watts, George F., *The Minotaur, 15*
Wedding Procession, Bridal Couple at Center, black-figured lekythos, **39**
wine, 36–37
woman, in ancient Greece, 38–39
Women Bearing Grave Offering, white-ground lekythos, 27
Wrestlers, **33**
writing activities, 67

Zeus, 16, 18
zodiac signs, 43